HAVE I TOLD YOU LATELY THAT I LOVE YOU?

REGINA G. MIXON

Copyright © 2014 by Regina G. Mixon
All rights reserved. In accordance with the U.S. Copyright Act of 1976, the scanning, uploading, and electronic sharing of any part of this book without the permission of the publisher is unlawful piracy and theft of the author's intellectual property. If you would like to use material from the book other than for review purposes), prior written permission must be obtained by contacting the publisher @info@regsbooks.org.

REGS Books LLC
P. O. Box 5397
Torrance, CA 90510

www.regsbooks.org

Printed in the United States of America

First Edition: August 2014

The publisher is not responsible for websites (or their content) that are not owned by the publisher.
All scriptures quoted are KJV unless specified otherwise.

Library of Congress Cataloging-in-Publication Data
Mixon, Regina G. 1957-
Have I Told You Lately That I Love You/Regina G. Mixon
Includes bibliographical references
ISBN978-0-9820699-8-1
1. Awareness 2. God's love 3. Types of love 4. Self-help

This book is dedicated to

God, first and foremost;

To my wonderful team at REGS Books:
There is no way I could do what I do without
you and your total support.

And to my daughter, who is also the most important
part of my team,

Emily Nicole Mixon

You inspire me and make me want to go to higher
heights.

You've endured much over the last 15 years or so
as I
pursued my visions and dreams.

I never could have or would have made it without
you.

Contents

Acknowledgments

Introduction

Chapters…

1. **What is Love?**
   - **Attributes & Characteristics of Love**
   - **Types of Love**
2. **Why Should We Love?**
3. **Who Should We Love?**
4. **When Should We Love?**
5. **Where Should We Love?**
6. **How Should We Love?**
7. **Living Up to Others Expectations**
8. **Have I Told You Lately That I Love You?**
9. **So What Is Love Again?**

Closing Thoughts

Prayer

References/Recommended Readings

"People are starving for love; not just hungry, but starving: Feed them."

Acknowledgements

Thank you to:

Michelle Shannon, my social media manager

Pam Nordberg, my editor

Dr. Netreia Carroll, my book cover designer, and

Irina Kolef with Bella Printing of Glendale.

HAVE I TOLD *YOU* LATELY THAT I LOVE YOU?

Introduction

Love is one of the most powerful words in the universe yet there are many myths surrounding what this simple word really means. I've heard countless times from various people throughout my life: "I love you." What has been most amazing to me is that with some, few or very few corresponding actions support the words spoken.

This book delves deeper into the subject matter. In each chapter in this book I will give some illustrations or examples and let you, as the reader, decide if genuine love is expressed. Of course, I will express my beliefs as to whether or not it is, but I ask that you draw your own conclusions.

The argument has been made countless times that people expressed their own version of love, but is that really true? It's true in the sense that perception becomes, or is, our reality. What do I mean by that? If the giver perceives themselves to be showing true love to someone then it is their reality. Is love really, I mean really, being shown, though?

When asked the question:—"What is love?" many of us will immediately respond with, "God is love." So true however, God tells us more about love in His Word and gives us the attributes of love, how we are to love, who we are to love, what love is, and the benefits of loving others and so forth. I will expound on that more in this book.

The primary scripture reference will come from 1 Corinthians 13. I will include other scriptures as well to support my conclusions and to allow me to say to each of you with boldness—"I love you!"

People use many names for love. We've heard some of them like—

- Puppy love
- Tough love
- Self-love
- Agape love
- Brotherly love
- Philia
- Eros
- Storge
- Thelema
- Infatuation
- Romantic Love
- Maternal Love
- Paternal Love
- Conditional Love
- Unconditional Love

- Companionate Love

I will expound more on some of these in these writings.

Though names for love, are any of these the true essence of what love is? Picture this scenario. I'll lay the foundation for you. Barbara has recently met Mike and has become quite smitten with him. Mike, on the other hand, is the playboy type and is not interested in or looking for a real relationship. After a few weeks of dating, their conversation goes something like this:

Mike: Hey Barbara. Baby you know we've been dating for six weeks now. Don't you think it's time we take it to the next level?

Barbara: I don't know, Mike. It's still too soon, and I'm honestly saving myself for the man I'm going to marry. (Secretly hoping Mike is the one and asks for her hand in marriage. She's desperate.)

Mike: Well baby I really believe I love you. I know it's only been a little while but what we have is special. I believe you're the one.

Barbara: Oh I think you're the one too! (Smiling) I just need to know.

Mike: Baby, how will we really know if we don't take it to the next level?

STOP! Is this love? Is this any form of love? If so, please tell me what kind of love it is. It doesn't take a rocket scientist to see what Mike really wants. And Barbara is obviously so desperate in her need or desire to have someone in her life she does not even see all of the signs.

Oh yeah, he told her he loves her. Big deal! Don't fall for it girlfriend. I'm here to tell you it is not love.

Scenario 2: A mom and her young adult children are having a discussion about respecting and fully supporting each other. The discussion is spearheaded by the mom and specifically geared to get them to come together, pray together, work together, play together, and become the best that each of them can be by not doing solo acts but working together. (I know this one sounds familiar to some. Rest assured, I am not talking about you. This is only an example.) Her only goal in all of this is to do as the Word says--bringing a divided house together so God can get the glory from their lives and for generations to come.

Mom: Okay, let's discuss how we can truly respect, support and help each other to be the best that we can be collectively and individually. And, once we do that how can we enlarge our territory by helping others?

Children (daughter taking the lead): Here we go again (heavy sigh). Who do you know that meets every week to discuss these types of things? None of my friends and their families do. This is too much!

Mom: Successful families, that's who! (Anger starting to rise) Is it wrong to want to see us all succeed? (Fire blowing from nostrils now.) I tell you!

Children (son now speaking): Well, I can only give you about fifteen to thirty minutes, as I have a ballgame to go to and I know I'll be busy next week.

Mom (totally exasperated now): Just forget it! Just forget it all! I am through!

In this example, did you feel any love coming from any of them? This is a tricky one as what is demonstrated is a lack of respect, frustration, anger, and all kinds of negative emotions. This does not mean the family does not love each other, it merely means no acts were shown. Or were there?

Amos 3:3 asks the question, "Can two walk together except they agree?" Matthew 12:25 states a house divided against itself shall not stand.

The mother in the scenario understands and recognizes the importance of coming together in agreement. She shows love initially by being concerned about not only her success but the success of her household. She fully understands her role as a teacher which requires her to train her children in the right way so they can do the same with their young. But, she lost it herself.

Throughout the book I will give similar illustrations. As you read them, please don't laugh too hard or be too critical. If you're honest you will see yourself and/or someone you know in the writings. The characters are fictional, but they very well could be you.

Let's get into the meat and potatoes now. Let's feed on and chew on some good food for nourishment and growth.

Chapter One

What *is* Love?

"Though I speak with the tongues of men and of angels, but have not charity (love), I am become as sounding brass, or a tingling symbol: And though I have the gift of prophecy, and understand all mysteries and all knowledge; and though I have all faith, so that I could remove mountains, and have not charity (love), I am nothing. And though I bestow all my goods to feed the poor, and though I give my body to be burned, and have not charity (love), it profiteth me nothing." I Corinthians 13:1-3

Love, oh love, that magical, mystical word used so often by many. "I love you" is something that people toss around so loosely without realizing the full implications of that one powerful word or statement. So, what exactly is love? That is the question I hope to answer in this chapter.

Webster's Concise Dictionary defines love as—

1. A strong, tender affection; deep devotion, as to one's child, parent, etc.
2. The affection felt by two persons who are sexually attracted to one another
3. A person who is the object of another's affection
4. A very great interest or fondness
5. A god of love, as Cupid or Eros

The New Webster's Concise Dictionary of the English

Language. 2003 Edition

That's how Webster's defines it, but let's delve a bit deeper into the subject matter. I'm sure you noticed, as I did, that affection was mentioned in three of the five definitions shown above. You'll read more as to why I believe this is important in later chapters.

Love has been called many things—the universal language; a many splendored thing, and the French even call it L'amour!

Kenny Rogers sings the song, "Have I Told You Lately That I Love You?"

This song was written as a prayer although it's commonly used at weddings.

Brian Hinton, author, poet and musicologist stated it is considered one of the finest love songs of the country. This song describes the awesome, wonderful love of God.

I encourage you to locate, read, and re-read the lyrics. I believe you will be inclined to agree with Hinton and declare this one of the finest love songs ever. This song describes the awesome, wonderful love of God.

Again, you might say, and even the Bible tells us, that God is love; and you would be correct. For the sake of these writings, we go into this with a clear understanding that this is the absolute truth—no ifs, ands, or buts. I will, however, delve just a bit more into what love is.

Attributes and Characteristics of Love

1. Love is long-suffering
2. Love is patient
3. Love is kind
4. Love is not envious
5. Love does not parade itself
6. Love is not puffed up
7. Love does not behave rudely
8. Love does not seek its own
9. Love is not provoked
10. Love thinks no evil
11. Love does not rejoice in iniquity (wickedness)
12. Love rejoices in truth
13. Love bears all things
14. Love believes all things
15. Love hopes all things
16. Love endures all things

I Corinthians 13

Wow! The Bible says a whole lot more about love than Webster's! Are you sure you really mean it when you say you love someone? Really?

Let's make a comparison between the two—Webster's deals mostly with affections or feelings while the Bible deals with acts or behaviors. This book deals with both, as the two go hand-in-hand.

Let's take a look at some of the types of love or common terms we use to describe love. I mentioned some of these in the introduction. In this chapter I will list some and tell you a little as to what each of them are or are considered to be.

Types of Love

1. Puppy Love—A childish, innocent temporary crush on someone that you don't know well.*
2. Tough Love—A love that is expressed by setting boundaries for the good of the other person.*
3. Self-Love—A positive feeling that one has about who they are and what they deserve. This is often expressed by treating yourself well, respecting yourself, wanting yourself to be happy and expecting others to respect you too.*
4. Agape—The highest of the four types of love in the Bible. Agape love indicates the nature of God toward His beloved Son, toward the human race generally, and toward those who believe on the Lord Jesus Christ. Agape love conveys God's will to His children about their attitudes toward one another. Agape love expresses the essential nature of God.***

5. Brotherly Love—Having a feeling of love for your neighbor, because all humanity is considered to be a part of a larger family of human beings.* The phrase is used in a symbolic sense to express love of Christians for one another; love for the broader brotherhood of true believers, for the members of the church, the household of faith.***
6. Philia—Friendship in Modern Greek, a dispassionate, virtuous love. It includes loyalty to friends, family and community and requires virtue, equality and familiarity. Philia means affectionate regard or friendship in both ancient and Modern Greek.
7. Eros—Passionate love, with sensual desire and longing. Eros does not have to be sexual in nature.
8. Storge—Means "affection" in ancient and modern Greek. It is the desire to do something, to be occupied, to be in prominence. It is natural affection, like that felt by parents for offspring.**

Definitions annotated with * taken from Dr. Paulette Kouffman Sherman, NY Love Examiner—15 Different Types of Love

Definitions annotated with ** taken from Wikipedia, Greek words for love

Definitions annotated with *** taken from www.christianity.about.com

These are some of the most common types of love we hear of, so let's inject a scenario or two. Can you identify the type of love that's being exhibited? Keep in mind the definitions of love.

Sam: Hi Ron! Beautiful day, isn't it?

Ron: Yeah it is, but I just found out my brother in Texas passed. Man, I don't have the resources to even go for the funeral. I lost my job two weeks ago and didn't even see it coming. They had a massive layoff. My family is really struggling now!

Sam: Don't worry about it man. Let's sit and talk a minute. I believe together we can make this happen.

Do you believe love was shown, and if so, what kind? Was more than one type displayed?

Take a look now at Ruth and Dianne's conversation:

Ruth: Girl, I have been looking for you! (Not waiting for a response, she rushes on) I've been so blessed lately! I came into a huge, I mean HUGE sum of money, and I have been shopping until I drop. Bought me a new car, a house, tons and tons of clothing, shoes, and jewelry--you name it, I bought it for MYSELF! Oh girl, enough about me, though-- What you been up to?

Dianne: Ruth, my luck couldn't be worse! I'm so happy for you, though. (Dianne is a Christian and sincerely is happy for Ruth.) My family and I are almost homeless.

Can you believe my husband decided he would up and leave? And to make matters worse, he left us penniless--I mean penniless. He closed the bank accounts, cancelled my credit cards. Oh girl, I just never thought he would do this to me and the boys! I give and give and never ever thought we'd be in this position. But you know what? In spite of it all, God is good and I trust that He will meet every need the kids and I have. I'm STILL trusting God, and He will bring us through it. I know He will!

Ruth: Dianne, it was so good to see you. I really hate the predicament you and the kids are in. Men! I'm gonna pray for you and yours. God's going to see you through this. Gotta run. Smooches!

Dianne: Thanks for your prayers. Again, I am so happy for you, and yes, I know God will make a way. I have faith!

Do you know any Ruth's? Now don't go naming them, but I'm sure we all know at least one. What type love was displayed here? Look at this closely, as your first thought may be none. That wouldn't be correct.

Dianne, although going through hardship, was genuinely happy for Ruth. Don't just look at the actions or statements of Ruth; look also to Dianne to see how she responded. Did Dianne show love?

In the final scenario for this chapter-- well let me set this up—Devin and his twin brother, Kevin have come together after being estranged for many years. Devin has been battling with drugs for the longest time. Kevin tried and tried to help him and finally decided he had had enough.

Kevin allowed Devin to stay with him several times and each time Devin robbed either Kevin personally or his children of something—money, stereos, games; whatever wasn't nailed down, Devin took.

Devin now wants to stay with Kevin again. Disheveled and breathing hard, he approaches Kevin and the conversation goes like this:

Devin: Hey bro, I need a place to crash again. I know we haven't seen each other in a long time but I promise you now that I am clean. I haven't used drugs in months. I just need a place to stay for a while.

Kevin: Bro, you know I love you much, but I can't allow you to come into my home again. I trusted you time and time again. Man, I almost lost my family behind your shenanigans. My wife threatened to leave me if I ever allow you to stay again and that's not going to happen. Besides, it's obvious you're still using. You're filthy!

Devin: Man, I swear I'm clean! C'mon, just let me stay for a few nights. I promise I won't take anything.

Kevin: Like I said, I can't and I won't allow you to stay. What I will do for you, though is take you to a rehab place that I know about. They can help you. You can stay there, go through their treatment program, and get clean but you cannot stay with us.

Did Kevin display love for his brother? After all, Devin swore that he was not on drugs and that he would not take anything. He just wanted and needed a place to sleep (or so he said). What kind of love was shown?

"Love—not dim and blind but so far-seeing that it can glimpse around corners, around bends and twists and illusion; instead of overlooking faults love sees *through* them to the secret inside." Vera Nazarian, *Salt of the Air*

I've told you some about what love really is in this chapter. In the following chapters, I will address the who, what, when, where, why, and how's to loving.

I will not cover infatuation, romantic love, companionate love, maternal love, paternal love, divine love, unconditional love and conditional love in any great detail in this writing; however, I do suggest you explore on your own the meaning of each of these.

Do you know what love is now after reading this chapter? Don't be too quick to answer yes as there's more—much, much more.

*Love is as simple as the absence of self given to another. God, when invited, fills the void of any unrequited love; hence loving is how one is drawn closer to God, no matter its most horrific repercussions.
Chris Jami, Venus in Arms*

Chapter 2

Why Should We Love?

"A new commandment I give unto you, that ye love one another as I have loved you, that ye also love one another. By this shall all men know that ye are my disciples, if ye have love one to another. John 13:34-35

This particular subject is relatively simple—scripture tells us to do so, as referenced in John 13:34-35. That is the main reason why we should love. There are also more benefits to loving others.

Karma, what goes around comes around-- the boomerang effect, are words and phrases used in essence to state that whatever one gives out returns to them. Well, the Word even tells us to give and it shall be given unto us—pressed down, shaken together, and running over shall men give into our bosoms.

Even unbelievers understand and apply this biblical principal. It behooves those that profess to be Christians to fully understand why we are to love and aggressively seek to live or walk this out in our daily lives. We are, after all, supposed to be light and the example.

There are numerous scriptures in the Bible that tell us why we are to love. One in particular is Matthew 25, where Jesus clearly states when we have exhibited acts of love by helping those in need, we have done it unto Him. That alone is reason enough to look for someone daily to *show* love.

"But really, are there more reasons as to why we should love? I mean it's good and all telling me what the Bible says, but why should I just love people? Many of them don't even seem to care at all about me"

Allow me to state that there are so, so many benefits to loving. People all over are hurting and if you've queried some you will find that the number one reason they hurt is not feeling or believing they are loved.

Too many wear masks—the smile plastered on their faces hiding the deeply seated pain within.

Far too many isolate themselves, as they think in doing so they are actually insulating themselves from further hurts and pains.

There are those that have committed suicide; those that don't live up to their full potential because deep down inside they have not, or do not, believe they are loved.

Why should you love someone? After all, you yourself, truth be told, are in need of love. You're hurting and no one seems to care or show any expressions of love toward you. No one cares about your plight, your issues, you and your family. More often than not, people completely ignore you. *"So, why, please tell me why I should love those that don't even seem to care about me."*

That, my friend, is the very reason you should show love--you know the hurts, you've felt the pains. Give it away and let it boomerang back to you. Yes, it may seem like it takes forever for anyone to even notice you but one guarantee I give you—it WILL come back. Maybe not in the way you expect it or not in the people you expect it from but it WILL come back. That bears repeating again--it WILL come back. Say to yourself, "As I give love or show love to others, I trust completely that God will send someone in to give and show love to me and mine in our time of need. I believe this to be true." Remember, give and it shall be given unto you.

Keep in mind the many different aspects and attributes of love; there are many different types of love, as evidenced by those shown in Chapter 1. Knowing which type of love to be used in any given situation often requires much prayer and discernment. In my opinion, the worst thing a person can do is believe from the bottom of their heart that they are showing love to someone and preface it with fakeness, phoniness, or some other action that leaves the intended recipient not feeling loved, but confused.

I want you to take a moment or two and think back to a time you were in desperate need of love and understanding. Let your mind roam to one specific situation that you perhaps prayed and prayed over, and even though you knew God loved you, you desired some sort of consolation from a human.

Can you see it? How did you feel? Let's continue--Now in this particular situation no one came for you. Perhaps someone did, but you had been burned and wounded so many times before that when asked "How are you doing?" your immediate response was "I'm fine."

Hurting, broken, desperately in need of love, lying to yourself and to others, dealing with serious trust issues, emotionally wounded, spiritually wounded, trying continually to give out to others what you "think" they need or even what you yourself need, a total wreck, betrayed by family, friends, church, suffering silently from the loss of a job, the loss of a loved one, the loss of your home, the loss of family and friends, yet you respond, "I'm fine." Liar!

Now imagine in your mind that friend, that co-worker, that pastor, that family member, that boss, that neighbor—all going through their pains, similar to ones you've experienced or are going through. So you tell me—why should we love?

Chapter 3

Who Should We Love?

Going back now to the scriptures, Jesus said the greatest commandment is this—Thou shalt love the Lord thy God will all of our heart, mind, and soul and thou shalt love thy neighbor as thyself. Who should we love?

God First

You Next

Your Neighbor

Sounds pretty simple doesn't it? You know what—it really can be. It will take work and a conscious effort on your part but it can be done.

God First

Loving God should be our very first desire and priority. Remember the song—"Jesus loves me this I know, for the Bible tells me so"? He does love you and loving Him should be your main priority.

God is love and He is so awesome! His love is absolutely 100% unconditional. Wow! Got to love someone who has that much love for you! How can you not?

You Next

The second greatest commandment is this, we should love our neighbor as we love ourselves.

In order to fulfill this commandment, we *must* first love ourselves. How can one love their neighbor as they love themselves without first LOVING yourself? Impossible to do!

In Chapter 6, I'll discuss how we are to love God first, then ourselves and our neighbors. Please allow me a moment though to interject here that it is all doable. Otherwise it would not be in the Word.

While reading this, stay open to the possibility of making some course corrections and/or course changes and you will be ready for a revival of love—a revival of the Bible—like never before.

So back we go to conclude this part; loving yourself, really loving yourself opens the door for you to fulfill the last part of this commandment, which is--

Love Your Neighbor as You Love Yourself

This concludes the trinity—God, you, your neighbor. I know by now you are asking—"Who is my neighbor?" Believe it or not, the Bible even gives an answer for that.

Jesus often spoke in parables. When confronted with the question, He gave the parable we often refer to as "The Parable of the Good Samaritan." He describes a situation where a person had fallen and was injured and three different people passed by him. The first two took a quick look at the man, assessed the situation and decided that he was not important enough, or the situation was not serious enough, for them to attend to his needs. They went on their way to do whatever it was they were set out to do. They couldn't and wouldn't be bothered by this man's situation.

Thank God the third passerby came along! He not only stopped and assessed the situation, saw the man was truly hurt and in need of help, BUT also provided the aid needed.

You might say that he went out of his way to help a total stranger that was in need, and you would be right.

After taking him to a place where he could get the help needed, he took it a step further and told them if the stranger incurred any additional debt to put it on his account and he would pay it when he returned or came back through again.

First off, this man had to be one of character and integrity! In order for to promise to pay the caregiver, they had to believe he was trustworthy and would hold true to his word.

How many of you today can honestly look at yourself and know that if you were in this situation and said this to a care provider that the services would be provided or honored? The world has really changed and sometimes not for the better. That's why we have to get back to the basics—living and loving according to the Word of God. Our words should mean something.

In days long gone, a man could and would give a handshake to seal a deal. That doesn't work anymore.

Again, we have to get back to being people of character and integrity, people whose actions correspond to the words spoken. We must get back to this!

Now, this Good Samaritan was obviously one that loved God and himself: he was compassionate, confident, did not feel threatened in any way by the man's condition, didn't feel that he was being taken advantage of—he simply saw a need and met it. That is a man after God's own heart.

It doesn't take a rocket scientist to figure out in each of these scenarios who the neighbor was. But for those that have not figured it out, the man lying by the side of the road was the neighbor and the Good Samaritan loved him as he so obviously loved himself.

To recap, it's vital, crucial we love God first, ourselves second, and then our neighbors.

Your neighbor could be someone living in the same neighborhood as you. Your neighbor could be someone living thousands of miles away. Your neighbor could be someone you know, or as shown in the parable, a total stranger. Your neighbor could be a family member, a friend, and sometimes—yes, drum roll—even an enemy or a perceived enemy.

Your neighbor can be a wayward child, a struggling mom, an aspiring entrepreneur--it can be anyone.

Stay open and look for ways to spot and assist or love your neighbor.

Remember, be careful how you treat strangers, as you may be among angels unaware. There may just be angels in your midst and you don't even see them.

I'll close this chapter with something I've heard countless times. The question posed is what if Jesus came to your house? How would you treat Him? Well, the reality of it is—and notice these are my beliefs—I believe Jesus comes by quite often and is rejected. What does He look like?—any of those people shown above--that's who. That is something to think about.

> *Anyone who does not love does not know God, because God is love. I John 4:8 ESV*

Chapter 4

When Should We Love?

I know you are throwing up your hands saying—"Me, me! I know." This is an easy one—we should love at all times. Yes, at ALL times!

When should we love? When we feel like it--when we don't feel like it (feelings can be fickle anyway). We should love when we're challenged in loving someone, as their actions may show that they do not want or desire any love from you. Don't look at what you think you see; keep showing and expressing love to them. Helen Baylor sings the song, *"Love Brought Me Back."* Read her autobiography in *"No Greater Love: The Helen Baylor Story."* And love them! Love them in spite of them.

We should show expressions of love daily. As long as there is breath in our bodies, we should constantly look for ways to show someone some love. As we awaken to a new day, one of our first thoughts should be--to whom can I show love today? That should be a part of our daily prayers.

I believe it's most important to show some form of love each and every day in some form or fashion.

When should we love? When we see a brother or sister in need is a good time. Another parable Jesus spoke is, "I was hungry and you fed me; naked and you clothed me; in prison and you visited me." He was asked—when did we do this? His response was, "When we have done it unto the least of them, you have done it unto me."

From this parable we see examples of both who we should love as well as when we should love. People are hungry, literally starving for love; feed them. People are naked and imprisoned (even if only in their minds); clothe them with love, visit them.

When we see someone in need is the very time we should demonstrate love. Don't look at the need, assess it and decide you're not the one to meet it; decide you just may be the one to do so.

Do not look at a person in need, knowing full well you have the ability to meet the need and give them what so many give—ineffective words. "I'm praying for you." "Well, if nothing has come through later, I may be able to help you." "God bless you sister."

We've all heard these at some point in our lives. Love is ACTION! Let's reverse the letters in action and change it to—I Act On! *I Act On* helping to meet your needs now. *I Act On* assisting you in any and every way I can NOW! I Act On--I Act On--I Act On! Action!

When should we love? The time is always now. Saying I'll pray for you, God bless you or any other clichés we have down pat does not help if one's house is on fire.

Giving one a good ole "God bless you" doesn't mean a thing if one is sick and in need of immediate medical attention. Screaming and shouting to the heavens on one's behalf when they're faced with eviction, in need of clothing or some other material thing, in need of shelter--just in need period means absolutely nothing! Maybe, just maybe, when you're confronted with a situation like this you will begin to think that MAYBE God sent you their way so that you could be a help to them. Maybe He supplied you with the resources to help in the areas needed and even whispered in your ears: "I want you to help him/her." Could it be? That's something to think about, huh?

And even with all of this, you decide--well, I'll just pray for them. The scripture says "Today if you hear My voice, harden not your hearts." Key words—"Today" and "harden not."

When should we love? I told you I would say it a both the beginning and the end—we should love at all times. Today is the day!

Chapter 5

Where Should We Love?

Just about any old place will do! Think about it, you may be inspired or moved to love or show love to someone while at the **Laundromat**, minding your own business, washing and folding your clothes. Suddenly, out of nowhere you see someone, a total stranger even, and your heart tugs at you that you need to offer some help. Love=I Act On or Action—remember?

This person is having a difficult time doing their laundry. What comes easy for you—the folding of and placing your clothes in a basket—seems to be a real struggle for them. Now most people wouldn't even notice this or stop to ask how they can assist this person. Maybe it is fear that the person won't accept help but your inner man is saying—help her. What stops you? You may just be the answer to her prayer.

Perhaps you're spending a day **shopping** and notice someone counting out change to see if they have enough to pay for their items. You're blessed and have more than enough to pay for your items and take care of your needs. This is a good place to show love by performing an act of kindness toward the person.

We often look for those outside our homes or outside of our **immediate family** to express love to, but what about looking at what you can do to show love to this group of people? Don't forget as you are going about showing it to others, let it begin at home! You've heard the phrase—charity (love) begins at **home** and then spreads abroad.

Look for, become an undercover agent, looking for, identifying and meeting the needs of those in your own home--in your own family first.

Going back to love, expressions of love, and types of love--always pray to see which form of love needs to be given in any and all situations.

Okay, church lady, you go to church Sunday after Sunday, to Wednesday night Bible studies, to Saturday choir rehearsals—any time the doors are open, you are there. Oh, to be close to God is your prayer; and what better place than spending time with all of your brothers and sisters in Christ. (Don't get me wrong, there is absolutely nothing wrong at all with this. I am just setting up a scenario of possibly missed opportunities to help.)

Do you realize that there are so many within the churches that are in need and hurting? Remember the church is a hospital for hurting people. Many come there to find solace, comfort and help.

Sister Mary really, I mean *really* loves the Lord. She loves her church. Hard times have fallen on her. She either can no longer drive due to her advanced age and/or her car may have broken down, maybe both, but something prevents her from getting there as she desires.

You are well aware of her situation, yet every service you go in your nice car—alone—and you pray that God blesses Sister Mary to be able to come to church as she desires. You repeatedly *say t*o her—*"Oh, Sister Mary, I am praying for you."* Sister Mary's hurting and a bit confused.

Yeah, so she lives fifteen minutes from you in the opposite direction of the church. Yes it would cause you to have to get up earlier, get dressed earlier than you had planned, and go fifteen minutes out of your way, BUT showing love means I Act On!

Church is a great place to help those hurting. You might think—"Well, Sister Mary can ride the church bus." You may even think—"Humph, she's got family who should be willing to get her to and from church." Hold up! Wait a minute! Aren't you her family member?

Let's go now to the **schools**. We want the school officials—teachers, principals, aides, cafeteria workers, maintenance and security-- to all look after the safety and well-being of our children. We want them to educate, watch over, protect, and feed our children. Has the thought ever crossed your mind that you can do something to help?

Volunteer! Do story time. Get involved. Help them to help you to help your child as well as all of the others in their classrooms.

Community Organizations. Yet another great place to show love. Many organizations fail due to lack of support from those within the communities they tirelessly work and strive to serve. Look for an organization whose mission and vision is near and dear to your heart and then get involved! Your steps in doing so may be the catalyst that helps the organization thrive and survive.

Don't sit on the sidelines complaining about all the wrongs in the world, in the community. Get involved! Become an active board member. Volunteer. Be passionate, not lackadaisical—be committed. Scripture says whatever we do we are to work as if we are working unto the Lord. Provide positive input. Be a team player. Give it your absolute best!

I'm sure by now you're thinking that this is work! Ah! You have just had an "aha" moment, as it really is. Love is work. Love is action. Love says and shows that I show up—I Act On!

To recap, just where should we love—home, immediate family, church, Laundromat, stores, schools, community organizations, extended family—just any ole place will do.

This is just a partial list of some places we can show love. Be creative and think of others. I'm so sure you'll see there is opportunity everywhere.

Love—Action--I Act On!

Chapter 6

How Should We Love?

Ah, how should we love? This question is one again that can be quite tricky. Looking at the past illustrations, one might think—"I know the answer." and you just might. For the sake of those who don't know, I write to you.

How we should love is largely determined by the situations we find ourselves faced with. We know we are to love as God loves—unconditionally—that's a given. But how or what other ways should we express love?

To clarify, God loves us unconditionally; however He also appropriately applies or shows different types of love when dealing with us. For example, when we are not walking in line with His will and His way for us, He chastises us. You heard me right! God will sometimes whip us into obedience. Don't confuse this with His forcing His will on us. That He would never do! But, He will whip us in line— for those that will heed His voice.

God sometimes leads us into the wilderness. What? Why would God do that? In order for us to come fully to the realization that we need Him, we cannot get along without Him, to get us to the point of obedience and total reliance upon Him; to get us to the point or to prepare us to minister to the needs of others. Yes, God loves us unconditionally; however, the promises of God are for those that are **willing** and **obedient,** and sometimes to get us to that point, He loves us enough to allow us to go through difficult circumstances.

Now you're asking the question—what does that have to do with how I should love?

Let's go back a few pages. When looking at ways to love a person, we should always take into consideration the need. There are many different ways to express love, as evidenced by the above paragraph which shows some of the ways God loves us. One just has to pray about the situation, assess it and make sure you are giving the individual the love that is needed at that time.

Keep in mind the different types of love. If you are giving, or trying to give, romantic love when what is actually needed at that time is tough love, you are not truly expressing or giving the love that is needed at that particular time. Discernment is key.

I personally pray that no one misreads my love need as I know in doing so, my need will still go unmet. If I am in need of truth and encouragement absent truth is provided, I still have an unmet need. If I am in need of guidance and direction and someone gives me food, my need is still unmet. If I am in need of food or shelter and clothing is provided, again the need is unmet. You get my point in all of this—first identify the need and then meet it.

In the scenario with Kevin and Devin in Chapter 1, you might believe that Kevin was too hard on Devin. You may have come to the conclusion that no love was shown. But taking a further look at the scenario, Kevin looked at and assessed the situation. Kevin did not give Devin what he wanted in the way of allowing him to stay with him and his family; however, Kevin gave Devin what he needed—a solution not only to his immediate need for shelter, but an opportunity to go and get himself together which would result in a permanent change. He offered love in the manner needed.

Yes, he was tough. He stood his ground and was firm. His "no" meant "no" but that doesn't negate the fact that he still expressed love for his brother by presenting him with viable solutions for his need.

How we should love someone does not always include giving the person what they say they need. If a person continually says over and over again that they are in need of money—well money may be the last thing that they need. Could it be that this particular person is in need of guidance or financial counseling in how to handle their finances? Could it be giving them money only puts a bandage on the real underlying problem? An alternative to repeatedly doling out your hard-earned money is suggesting they contact someone that deals with money management or helping them establish and maintain a budget.

Hard times can fall on any of us at any given time—that's a fact. The saying goes—we know where we've been but we don't know where we're going—and I am a living testimony that anything that can happen to anyone else can happen to you. No one is immune to life!

The saying goes—you give a person a fish and you've fed them that one time but if you teach them how to fish, you've fed them for a lifetime. Sometimes how we should love someone involves teaching them how to help themselves. "Help me to help you" should be the slogan for many as with "Together we can make it happen". We sometimes move too fast, although meaning well, and take on things that are not our crosses to bear. We go from helping to enabling. People need help, not enablement!

Let's go back to Chapter 1, in the scenario with Ruth and Dianne, Dianne did not specifically ask for help. She did mention her plight-- that was it. Dianne had fallen on hard times perhaps because her marriage had failed and she was unprepared for living life as a single parent. Reading a bit more into the story, maybe Dianne had given up her career, her hopes and her dreams of doing or becoming anything but a good wife and mother—to which she should be applauded as there is absolutely nothing wrong with that.

Now she finds herself in unfamiliar territory. Could Ruth have really taken the time to listen to hear what her needs were? Don't you think a better way, other than immediately dashing off likely thinking Dianne wanted money, was to hear her out? Could Ruth have offered to assist financially or provide her with connections, perhaps an agency or organization that deals with recently separated or divorced women with children? There are support groups out there for almost anything.

What Ruth did not do, in my opinion, was show any real love; she merely raced off to do more of chasing after material things. I wonder if Dianne felt any love or consolation after Ruth left. She likely felt that Ruth, along with many others, just didn't care.

How should we love? I ask that as you read you draw your own conclusions. Look at each situation separately. Don't try to lump Dianne's situation with someone similar and conclude that just like sister so-and-so Dianne is just whining or just like sister so-and-so Dianne is just looking for a handout. Oftentimes people are looking for a hand up, a listening ear, a caring soul, compassion, someone who can empathize with them, solutions, hope. *Silent* and *listen* are spelled using the same letters—the letters are just arranged differently. Listen with your ears. Listen with your heart. Listen to hear what the person is saying. Pray to hear what the spirit is saying and then listen to how the spirit leads, guides, and directs you to help the individual.

What if I don't hear the spirit? What if I'm not saved? What if I miss the moment? What if I get my signals crossed? It is okay. At least be receptive and I am sure you will hear what the person as well as the spirit is saying to you. When God means for us to help someone, He won't let you miss the opportunity. Again, that is if you are two things—willing and obedient.

Some have missed opportunities to love. I've had people share with me how a certain person constantly stayed on their minds and yet they kept putting off contacting the person. By the time they actually did, the person had expired or gone through a very serious ordeal and was in need of much help or consoling.

Some have shared with me how God led them to go and pray for the sick, and again they put it off. By the time *they* decided to do it, the person had transitioned and was no longer here with us. One person in particular shared that the Holy Spirit spoke and said to him—"What if your prayers and obedience had prolonged his life?" Listen people, listen!

How should I love people? I'll tell you what not to do—do not delay doing what you know you need to do as delaying may mean the end. Don't take time, people, or anything else for granted. The scripture says "Boast not about tomorrow for thou knowest not what a day may bring."

Finally, I go back to Chapter 1 with Mike and Barbara's scenario. Let me see the hands of those that know a few of these—desperate women and men on the prowl looking for their next victim. I have to say here in all seriousness, both of them are in need of help and truth be told, both are victims of what they have been taught, either by seeing it modeled, having it taught that this is the way a man or a woman should be, or just out of sheer ignorance.

How should they have shown love to each other? First of all, as a man, Mike should not have approached Barbara with the idea of having sex before marriage. They had been in a relationship for only six weeks! Six weeks is not long enough for anyone to really know someone! Even if it were, a real man would not do that.

And Barbara, poor Barbara! My heart goes out to her. I was Barbara and I personally know a lot of Barbara's—desperate, not just thirsty but dehydrated—who bought into that lie that having a piece of a man is better than having no man at all. Looking for love in all the wrong places, oh yes, Barbara was our name.

Alicia Keys sings the song, "A Woman's Worth." A part of the lyrics state—"cause a real man knows a real woman when he sees her--and a real man just can't deny a woman's worth." How did I get into this? I'm talking about how we should love and whether any expression of love shown in the previous examples!

Know your worth as an individual!

Concluding this chapter, suffice it to say, and I believe we can agree, no love was shown. Mike was looking for one thing and Barbara was secretly hoping for something altogether different as if marriage is the great cure-all. Please don't misread my passion for disdain or belittling marriage. I believe strongly in the institution of marriage according to the scriptures--what God has joined together--

How should we love? Look for the handwritings on the wall. Love God and yourself in a balanced way and ask Him to lead, guide, and direct you as to how to love others. Love fearlessly in whatever way you are led. And always remember, sometimes the best way we can love someone is to let them go. More of this will be explored in following chapters.

> *There is no fear in love, but perfect love casts out fear. For fear has to do with punishment,*

Chapter 7

Living Up to Others Expectations

"Regina, I've tried to love others: I really have! But sometimes their expectations of and from me are just too much! I give what I have but it's never enough. What do I do? And instead of them being grateful for what I've given, they continually ask for more, more, more. How can I continually show love, as I believe needs to be shown and as God has blessed me, when it's so obvious I am not living up to people's expectations of me?"

Does this sound like you? You've gone above and beyond in loving others and yet what you've done is often unappreciated, unacknowledged, and you are made to feel so, so small because—in that person's opinion—you still have not met the need or shown love. In essence, you are not living up to their expectations of what you should be doing—more, more, more, faster, faster, faster, harder, harder, harder.

This is something many of us confront on a regular basis. There are some, no matter how much you do or what you do, who will still want and demand more than what you have and/or are willing to give. Believe this, there are some that are hurting so bad that they feel the only way to feel good about themselves is when they are manipulating others, trying to get their sense of purpose from the lover, the giver.

There are some that have been extremely wounded by the vicissitudes of life; those that are looking for love from man that only God can give, that regardless of what you do or don't do, they never feel or believe it to be enough. It's impossible to live up to their expectations.

I've read, heard and experienced the saying—"Regardless of how much one gives, people will only remember the ONE thing you didn't do."

That's when one does what they can and then learns the gift of letting go as with the gift of a good old firm—No!

From time-to-time I'll watch the TV show *"How Lottery Changed My Life."* The stories are very interesting to me. Some went on to live their dreams which included supporting and helping others, but for others, the lottery winnings drove a wedge between the winner and his or her family.

On one particular episode, a man had won millions, had been very generous with his family members and had given to charities. Each day he would receive fifteen to twenty letters from people asking for money—many of the requests for unnecessary things.

Even though he had given to his family members, they still wanted more and more and it got to the point where he had to say no. So sad! All that he did was never enough. And when the show aired he stated that he and his mother and some siblings were not on speaking terms—all because of his winnings and their expectations.

I've heard both Oprah Winfrey and Steve Harvey say the same thing albeit maybe worded differently—that sometimes the best way to help one's family members that seek after money continually is to not be broke yourself.

Letting go can be extremely hard. In situations where it's obvious that people don't realize that God is their source and you are only one of many resources He has placed here to assist them, letting go may be the best act of love to display.

People who live their lives expecting everyone else to mend and make them whole creates the environment for those in their company to become codependents and enablers. Melody Beattie has several excellent books that deal with the issue of codependency—*"Codependent No More"*, *"Beyond Codependency"* and *"The Language of Letting Go"* to name a few.

Melody Beattie's official definition of codependency is: "*A codepedent person is one who has let another person's behavior affect him or her, and who is obsessed with controlling that person's behavior.*"

Several other experts define codependency as it relates to dealing with someone with an alcohol or drug addiction. In these writings, Melody's definition is used as it shows one can be codependent when dealing with *anyone*.

Taking a look again at the definition, can you think of perhaps one person that you have encountered in your lifetime with whom you were in a codependent relationship? As a parent, this is often our children; as a spouse, this can be your husband or wife; as an employer, this can be your employee; as a friend, this can be someone you truly care for—suffice it to say this can be one of any relationship you have with another.

In order to love as God desires and commands us to do, we must break the cycle of codependency. It likely requires us to know that there are many times we will not be able to nor should we try to live up to others expectations. It requires us to realize that by holding onto or enabling a loved one, we are delaying their healing as well as ours.

Although this book does not go into great details about the subject of codependency, I strongly encourage you to obtain books by other authors more knowledgeable than me regarding the subject, then read and apply all that you learn. You still love when you get to your point of healing: you love enough to set yourself free as well as the other party. You're helping both yourself and the other party grow and become the man and woman of God He intends us to be.

Whitney Houston's song, *"The Greatest Love of All."* has been a favorite of mine for many years. I absolutely love the lyrics! A part of it says—*"Learning to love yourself is the greatest love of all."* We have to learn to really love ourselves, be free, before we can ever give or show God's love to others. We have to be whole—nothing missing, nothing broken--and it can happen—it will happen!

How can I live up to others expectations and still be whole? I'm inclined to believe that most times I can't. I further believe it is not God's will for us to even attempt to live up to others' expectations but to strive daily to live up to His.

Another situation that comes to mind, and yes I've experienced this personally, is being overly committed. It is unreal the expectations that are placed upon those that have a willing heart, a desire to serve, a heart for the people! Whether it's on your job, in a business, at home, in church, wherever—when people see you really love the Lord and really desire to serve Him to the utmost, you will be asked to do things that others are unwilling and absolutely will not do for you.

People will impose their goals, visions, and dreams upon others without realizing that those people have so much going on in their own private lives. You will be asked to teach every class, attend every meeting, and sacrifice your time, talents and resources, to literally deny yourself and the needs of your home to fulfill *their* ambitions. Yes, I've been guilty as I tried to push some people to do that but you know what? Some had sense enough to say no. I later learned the power of "NO".

The harvest is plentiful and the laborers are few but we cannot overwork those that are already overloaded. Let's graciously accept help offered, ask others for help, accept the fact that many times people cannot give any more than they are giving, thank God for the help given during your time of need, and trust that He will send in the help needed a their time of need.

"Learning to have patience and not forcing the relationship is part of the twin soul process. If you are trying to force your will onto the other person, chances are you're not ready to really connect yourself. There should be no blame here—only deep and unconditional love." Chimnese Davids, My Unrequited Love Letters.

Don't try to force a relationship. Don't try to manipulate or control a relationship. Allow the other person to *be,* resulting in allowing yourself to just be. Eliminate blame. Do not, I repeat, do not attempt to enable someone, knowing the hurts it causes later. Giving deep and unconditional love, simply stated, is keeping the relationship in proper perspective—God first, you and your neighbor in a balanced way.

Yes, there will be times that you have to let go. There will be times when what appears to be tough love is applied and needed. There will be times you will shed tears as you truly desire to help another but can't. There will be times when you come to the full realization that the consequences of holding on prevents both you and the other party involved from living life the way God intended. There will be times when you're misunderstood. There will be times that many emotions will take place that cause you to wring your pillow throughout the day and night—weeping, sobbing—desperately wanting to please or in your mind, help people.

Remember, your number one goal in life is to please God. In doing so, even though you are unable to live up to a person's expectations, you know God only wants what's best for all of us.

How can you live up to others expectations? You can't! And I ask that from this day forward you decide that it is not the people you seek to please, but God. He's got this!

> *Codependency is the lack of having a life. A codependent does not have a life. A codependent in recovery is getting a life. A recovered codependent has a life. Author Melody Beattie*

> Don't try to force, manipulate, or control a relationship. Love enough to hold on when needed and let go when necessary.

Chapter 8

Have I Told You Lately that I Love You?

Seriously, have I told you lately that I love you? Hopefully I have by my actions and not necessarily the words spoken. The lyrics—"If I can just help somebody, as I travel through this land, then my living shall not be in vain" resonates within. It is my desire that those I've encountered in my lifetime know beyond a shadow of a doubt that they have been, and continue to be, loved by me.

That should be the desire of us all. Yes, when we meet the Master face-to-face, we want to hear—"Well done, thy good and faithful servant; you have finally finished your race." Loving others as God mandates in His Word is one sure way to know that we will hear those wonderful, sweet, soothing words, and we will enter into the rest of God.

Family is where love begins and ends. In loving others as God commands us, we daily add to the family. Love makes a family! We know that family is not always those in our own bloodlines, but rather those that are believers and embrace us into their lives.

Our family members are the ones who love and accept us for who we are and not for who they think we should be. The love of family is one of God's greatest gifts to us.

I refer to family a lot here. Just keep in mind that I am not talking about just our biological family members.

Family says and shows,—"I've got your back and I trust that you have mine as well." Family recognizes the importance of loving people, not enabling or hindering the works that God is doing in their lives.

Family members are the ones who would go to bat for you in a minute and defend you in the highest courts. They are those that encourage you to walk as they walk in loving God, loving yourself, and loving others.

Why am I stating so much about family when this chapter addresses the book's title? Because loving others should start with loving your immediate family first—"charity begins at home and then spreads abroad"—then, and only then, can one open themselves up to embracing, accepting and giving the love that is so desperately needed to others.

Yes, we should always begin with family.

Mark V. Olsen states—"At the end of the day, a loving family should find everything forgivable." Forgiveness is going to be necessary sometimes over and over again. It's a part of the loving process.

Significant Quotes Regarding Love

"Love can change a person the way a parent can change a baby--awkwardly, and often with a great deal of mess." Lemony Snicket

"Those whom we most love are often the most alien to us." Christopher Paolini

"Our family is a circle of strength of love with every birth and every union the circle grows." Unknown

"The love of a family is life's greatest blessings."

"Never forget the three powerful resources you always have available to you, love, prayer, and forgiveness." H. Jackson Brown, Jr.

"To forgive is to set a prisoner free and discover that the prisoner was you." Lewis B. Smedes

"You will know that forgiveness has begun when you recall those who hurt you and feel the power to wish them well." Lewis B. Smedes

"Accept the children the way we accept trees—with gratitude, because they are a blessing—but do not have expectations or desires. You don't expect trees to change: you love them as they are." Isabel Allende

"The only way love can last a lifetime is if its unconditional. The truth is this; love is not determined by the one being loved but rather by the one choosing to love." Stephen Kendrick, *The Love Dare*

As you read through some of the quotes, you will find that although dealing with love, forgiveness plays a huge role in loving. Why do you think that is? One of the many lessons I've learned in life is not only will we need forgiveness from others, but others will also require forgiveness from us. This can take place over and over again, often with the same ones.

We're all human and subject to let each other down. That's why when Jesus was posed with the question—"How many times should we forgive?" His response was seventy times seven a day. Now who is going to sit and actually count to see if they've reached the max? I know I'm not.

The Bible tells us love keeps no record of wrongs. I tell you the Bible sets the standards high for those of us that strive daily to walk as Jesus walked: there are some tall orders given us but the good news is—we can rise to the occasion.

Get a little bit radical with the love revolution! When wronged, before anyone even opens their mouth and asks for forgiveness, pray, and forgive them immediately. That's a powerful message in and of itself!

Sure, people will believe you to be strange but you are a chosen generation, a royal priesthood, a peculiar people. You are called out of darkness into the marvelous light. You are loved so much by God. You are well able to turn the other cheek. You can, when asked for an item of clothing, go the extra mile and give up a coat too. You are the righteousness of God, the seed of Abraham.

When you really start to daily walk in love, you won't even have to ask another the question—"Have I told you lately that I love you?" They will tell you how much you've shown them your love for them.

I close this section with a quote from Vera Nazarian (*The Perpetual Calendar of Inspiration*)

"Love is made up of three unconditional properties in equal measure:

1. Acceptance
2. Understanding
3. Appreciation

Remove any of the three and the triangle falls apart.

Which, by the way, is something highly inadvisable. Think about it—do you really want to live in a world of only two dimensions?

So, for the love of a triangle, please keep love whole."

A three-fold cord is not easily broken.

Have I told you lately that I love you?

Chapter 9

So What Is Love Again?

Prayerfully by now you know what love really is—I Act On—Action! Analogies have been used to prove a point that in any and all situations we can and should express love.

You've read the characteristics and attributes of love knowing that God is love. You've read and learned of some types of love that we, as humans, display toward each other.

You've read quotes and scriptures to further show you what love truly is.

ACTION! ACTION! ACTION!

Be it helping a brother or sister in need, applying tough love in situations deemed necessary to help another grow, being physically attracted to someone, showing love to yourself by establishing boundaries, or any number of things, remember you are acting on or taking action for the betterment of yourself as well as another.

A word of advice, when or if you find yourself in a position to show tough love to someone, pray about it and ask God to lead, guide, and direct you as to how to approach the person and the words you need to say. Doing it on your own may result in the individual feeling attacked as opposed to feeling the words and corresponding actions being done purely out of no other motive but love. Watch and pray!

What is love again! The French say "l'amour". The German call it "liebe". Italian says "Amore". The Filipino's call it "pagibig". The Irish call it "gra". The Spanish call it "amor" but regardless of what you call it, love is the key that makes the difference between death and life in so many cases.

Regardless of how it's pronounced verbally, when one shows another the love that they say they have for another person, there is no denying the love.

Love is truth. Be bold enough to tell someone the truth—in love. Don't sugarcoat it. Don't attack an individual; just tell the truth. The Bible tells us "And you will know the truth and the truth will set you free." John 8:32 ESV

Love is amazing! Love is absolutely awesome! Love is powerful! Love, oh love!

Closing Thoughts

After reading this, even with all of the humor included, it is my deepest desire and prayer that you no longer tell a person you love them, but rather express it in how you relate to that person. Love is a verb. Love is action. Love means "I Act ON." Love can be shown without uttering one single word.

Let's vow to live by the greatest example of all time—Jesus. Let us each take a look at our lives to see if our walk lines up with our talk. A truth I tell you, one can never go wrong in loving another. Yes, you *will be* totally and completely misunderstood by many. You will be rejected by some, praised by others, lied on and even talked about. I would be lying to you if I told you differently.

Don't succumb to the temptation to stop loving. Don't fall prey to the lies of the enemy that tells you someone is unlovable. Keep showing and expressing love in its various formats to whomever God places in your path. Remember Helen Baylor's song, "Love Brought Me Back." You never know the impact your expression of love may have on the life of someone. It can, and often does, result in touching and impacting the lives of many and has a boomerang effect as well. Whatever you give out comes right back at you. The life you save may be your own.

Don't go looking for love in all the wrong places. Remember, God first and He will lead you to the right places.

Don't believe that you're unlovable. I AM THAT I AM says that you are loved! Remember 1 Corinthians 13. Be a living example, a living testimony. Start a love revival!

There will be times when you'll have to love someone from afar. There will be times when you are taken advantage of and taken for granted. Remember, love never fails.

Don't become discombobulated or out of sorts if the ones you love don't show love in return or reciprocate. Understand why you are doing what you do and leave the rest in God's hands. God is ubiquitous and will always love you, and for every one that won't, He'll send in others that will. Your purpose for loving is so that men may see and glorify God. That's it!

Matriculate or grow in love. Plant seeds daily. Water them. Watch them grow. I'm sure you've heard—when you do for God what He cannot do for Himself, God will do for you what you cannot do for yourself.

Have I told you lately that I love you? Well, I'm saying it now, loud and clear—I LOVE YOU and there is nothing that you can do about it!

Please join me in praying the following prayer—asking God to allow His love to flow in and through us.

Prayer

"Father, I humbly bow before you today, thanking you for the love you have shown and continually show me. I thank you for forgiving me for all of my sins and loving me in spite of myself. Just as you love me, I know that you love others as you are no respecter of person. I pray that from this day forward you help me show unadulterated love to all I come in contact with. Help me to let my light shine before men so that they may see my good works and glorify you. Refill me daily as I empty myself by loving and serving you and others.

Create in me a clean heart and renew a right spirit within me.

From this day forward, I pray that you allow love to flow in and through me. I believe it and I receive it.

In Jesus' Precious Name,

Amen!"

References/Recommended Readings:

1. *Love*, The New Webster's Concise Dictionary of the English Language-Encyclopedic Edition 2003 Edition
2. "Greek words" Wikipedia.org/wiki,
3. *15 Different Types of Love—Dr. Paulette Kouffman Sherman*, Examiner.com, March 4, 2009
4. "Love in the Bible" About.com
5. *Tony and Lois Evans, "Seasons of Love"*— (Nashville, TN: Thomas Nelson 11/ 1998
6. The Holy Bible in the King James Version
7. Biblegateway.com
8. Van Morrison *"Have I Told You Lately that I Love You?"* performed by Kenny Rogers, 1989
9. *Melody Beattie, "Beyond Codependency"*-- (Self-published 07/2009)
10. *Melody Beattie, "The Codependent Parent"*— (San Francisco, CA: Harper Publishing, 06/1991)
11. *Helen Baylor, "No Greater Love: The Helen Baylor Story"*—(Harrisonburg, VA: Vision Publishing April 28, 2007)
12. *Barbara Cottman Becnel, "Codependent No More"*—(Center City, MN: Hazeldon Publishers, 11/1992)
13. *"Nelson's Illustrated Bible Dictionary"*— (Nashville, TN: Thomas Nelson Publishers, 1986)

Scriptural References:

1. "Thou shalt not avenge, nor bear any grudge against the children of thy people, but thou shalt love thy neighbor as thyself: I am the Lord." *Leviticus 19:18*
2. 'And thou shalt love the Lord thy God with all thine heart, and with all thy soul, and with all thy might. (vs 7) And thou shalt teach them diligently unto thy children, and shall talk of them when thou sittest in thine house, and when thy walkest by the way, and when thou liest down, and when thou risest up." *Deuteronomy 6:5- 7*
3. "But I say unto you, love your enemies, bless them that curse you, do good to them that hate you, and pray for them which despitefully use you, and persecute you. (Jesus speaking to the multitudes--the sermon on the mountains) (vs 46) For if ye love them which love you, what reward have ye? Do not even the publicans do the same?" *Matthew 5:44 & 46*
4. "Thou shalt love thy neighbor as thyself is recorded also in Matthew 19:19, 22:39, Galatians 5:14 and James 2:8
5. "Let love be without dissimulation. Abhor (hate) that which is evil; cleave to that which is good. Be kindly affectioned one to another with brotherly love; in honor preferring one another. *Romans 12:9-10*

6. "Love worketh no ill to his neighbor: therefore love is the fulfilling of the law." *Romans 13:10*
7. Galatians 5:16-23
8. Galatians 6:1-10
9. "If a brother or sister be naked, and destitute of daily food, And one of you say unto them, Depart in peace, be ye warmed and filled; notwithstanding you give them not those things which are needful to the body; what doth it profit?" James 2:15-16

About the Author

REGINA MIXON has been teaching the Word of God since 1988. She is the author of five books and has traveled to various locations throughout the United States speaking and teaching messages of encouragement primarily to women audiences. Regina is the mother of two grown children and makes her home in Carson, CA.

To contact the author, please write:

Regina Mixon
P. O. Box 5397
Torrance, California

Internet Address: www.regsbooks.org

Please include your testimony or help received from this book when you write. Your prayer requests are welcome.

BOOKS BY REGINA MIXON

To God be the Glory

Revised Edition—To God be the Glory—From Brokenness to Wholeness

Pursuing Your Purpose With Passion

Glory Wind Beneath My Wings

Reader's Testimonial

"I thought your book was good and thoughtfully compiled. Love is a concept we all can never hear enough of, and I appreciated the reminder about how we should be loving others and living in love. I liked the dialogues you included, especially interspersed with your more serious comments about love. Sometimes it's easier to learn about a concept through a dialogue, and these dialogues helped demonstrate your ideas. I also liked how you were straightforward in your charges of how, who, why, etc. we should love. You adequately challenged your readers!" Pam Nordberg

Notes

And the love revival begins!